I0447043

Congressional
Research
Service

Hydraulic Fracturing:
Chemical Disclosure Requirements

Brandon J. Murrill
Legislative Attorney

Adam Vann
Legislative Attorney

June 19, 2012

Congressional Research Service
7-5700
www.crs.gov
R42461

CRS Report for Congress ———————————————
Prepared for Members and Committees of Congress

Summary

Hydraulic fracturing is a technique used to free oil and natural gas trapped underground in low-permeability rock formations by injecting a fluid under high pressure in order to crack the formations. The composition of a fracturing fluid varies with the nature of the formation, but typically contains mostly water; a proppant to keep the fractures open, such as sand; and a small percentage of chemical additives. Some of these additives may be hazardous to health and the environment. The Shale Gas Production Subcommittee of the Secretary of Energy Advisory Board (SEAB) has recommended public disclosure, on a well-by-well basis, of all of the chemical ingredients added to fracturing fluids, with some protection for trade secrets.

Currently, no such law or regulation exists at the federal level. In his 2012 State of the Union Address, President Barack Obama said he would obligate "all companies that drill for gas on public lands to disclose the chemicals they use," citing health and safety concerns. In May 2012, the Bureau of Land Management (BLM) published a proposed rule that would require companies employing hydraulic fracturing on lands managed by BLM to disclose the content of the fracturing fluid. In addition, there have been legislative efforts in the 112th Congress. H.R. 1084 and S. 587, the Fracturing Responsibility and Awareness of Chemicals Act (FRAC Act), would create more broadly applicable disclosure requirements for parties engaged in hydraulic fracturing.

Chemical disclosure laws at the state level vary widely. Of the 15 laws examined in this report, fewer than half require direct public disclosure of chemical information by mandating that parties post the information on the FracFocus chemical disclosure website. The level of detail required to be disclosed often depends on how states protect trade secrets, as these protections may allow submitting parties to withhold information from disclosure at their discretion or to submit fewer details about proprietary chemicals, except, perhaps, in emergencies. Even if a disclosure law does not protect information from public disclosure, other state laws, such as an exemption in an open records law, may do so. States also have varying laws regarding the timing of these disclosure requirements.

This report provides an overview of current and proposed laws and regulations at the state and federal levels that require the disclosure of the chemicals added to the fluid used in hydraulic fracturing. **Appendix A** provides a glossary of many of the terms used in this report. **Appendix B** contains a table summarizing the fracturing chemical disclosure requirements described in this report. For an overview of the relationship between hydraulic fracturing and the Safe Drinking Water Act (SDWA), see CRS Report R41760, *Hydraulic Fracturing and Safe Drinking Water Act Issues*, by Mary Tiemann and Adam Vann.

Contents

Tables

Appendixes

Contacts

Introduction

Hydraulic fracturing is a technique used to free oil and natural gas trapped underground in low-permeability rock formations by pumping a fracturing fluid under high pressure in order to crack the formations.[1] The composition of a fracturing fluid varies with the nature of the formation, but typically contains mostly water; a proppant to keep the fractures open, such as sand; and a small percentage of chemical additives.[2] A primary function of these additives is to assist the movement of the proppant into the fractures made in the formation by reducing friction between the fracturing fluid and the pipe used to pump the fluid into the formation.[3] Although some of these chemical additives may be harmless, others may be hazardous to health and the environment.[4] A report by the minority staff of the House Committee on Energy and Commerce found that between 2005 and 2009, the 14 leading oil and gas service companies used "780 million gallons of hydraulic fracturing products" in fracturing fluids, with "95 of the products containing 13 different carcinogens."[5]

The Shale Gas Production Subcommittee of the Secretary of Energy Advisory Board (SEAB) has made several recommendations intended to address the effects of shale gas production on health and the environment.[6] One recommendation calls for the public disclosure, on a "well-by-well basis," of all of the chemical ingredients—"not just those that appear on Material Safety Data Sheets"—added to fracturing fluids, with some protection for trade secrets.[7] Proponents of chemical disclosure laws maintain that public disclosure would allow for health professionals to better respond to medical emergencies involving human exposure to the chemicals; assist researchers in conducting health studies on shale gas production; and permit regulators and others to perform baseline water testing to track potential groundwater contamination if it occurs.[8] However, some manufacturers of the additives, as well as others in the industry, remain reluctant to disclose what they consider to be proprietary chemical formulas, expressing concerns that they would lose their valuable trade secrets if competitors had access to them.[9]

This report provides an overview of current and proposed laws and regulations at the state and federal levels that require the disclosure of the chemicals added to the fluid used in hydraulic

---

[1] Department of Energy, Modern Shale Gas Development in the United States: A Primer, ES-4 (2009) [hereinafter Department of Energy Primer], *available at* http://www.netl.doe.gov/technologies/oil-gas/publications/epreports/shale_gas_primer_2009.pdf.

[2] *See id.* at 56, 61-64.

[3] *Id.*; Reservoir Stimulation §§7-6.2, 7-6.4 (Michael J. Economides et al. eds, 3d ed. 2000).

[4] Department of Energy Primer, *supra* note 1, at 62.

[5] Minority Staff of H. Comm. on Energy and Commerce, 112th Cong., Chemicals Used in Hydraulic Fracturing 5, 9 (2011) [hereinafter Minority Report on Fracturing Chemicals], *available at* http://democrats.energycommerce.house.gov/sites/default/files/documents/Hydraulic%20Fracturing%20Report%204.18.11.pdf.

[6] Department of Energy, Shale Gas Production Subcommittee Second Ninety Day Report 1 (2011), *available at* http://www.shalegas.energy.gov/resources/111811_final_report.pdf.

[7] *Id.* at 5-6, 17. Employers are required to use MSDSs to warn employees of certain hazardous chemicals in the workplace under the Occupational Safety and Health Act. *See* 29 C.F.R. §1910.1200.

[8] *See* Lisa Song, *Secrecy Loophole Could Still Weaken BLM's Tougher Fracturing Regs*, InsideClimate News, February 15, 2012, *available at* http://insideclimatenews.org/news/20120215/blm-fracturing-chemicals-disclosure-hydraulic-fracturing-proprietary-natural-gas-drilling.

[9] *See* Minority Report on Fracturing Chemicals, *supra* note 5, at 11-12.

---

fracturing. Currently, no such law or regulation exists at the federal level. In his 2012 State of the Union Address, President Barack Obama said he would obligate "all companies that drill for gas on public lands to disclose the chemicals they use," citing health and safety concerns.[10] In May 2012, the Bureau of Land Management (BLM) published a proposed rule that would require disclosure of the content of fracturing fluids used on lands managed by the agency. In addition, there have been legislative efforts in the 112th Congress. H.R. 1084 and S. 587, the Fracturing Responsibility and Awareness of Chemicals Act (FRAC Act), would create more broadly applicable disclosure requirements for parties engaged in hydraulic fracturing.

At the state level, the Interstate Oil and Gas Compact Commission, an organization with members that include state regulators and industry representatives, has argued that current regulation of hydraulic fracturing by the states is sufficient.[11] At least 15 states already have some form of chemical disclosure requirements. These provisions vary widely, but generally indicate (1) which parties must disclose information about chemical additives and whether these disclosures must be made to the public or a state agency; (2) what information about chemicals added to a fracturing fluid must be disclosed, including how specifically parties must describe the chemical makeup of the fracturing fluid and the additives that are combined with it; (3) what protections, if any, will be given to trade secrets; and (4) at what time disclosure must be made in relation to when fracturing takes place. Others states are in the process of considering disclosure laws or regulations.

For a glossary of some of the terms used in this report, see **Appendix A**. For a table summarizing the chemical disclosure laws and proposals described in this report, see **Appendix B**.

Federal Proposals

Bureau of Land Management Proposed Rule

In May 2012, BLM published proposed regulations governing the use of hydraulic fracturing technology by holders of oil and gas leases on federal lands managed by BLM.[12] The proposed rule established a number of disclosure and filing requirements for "well stimulation activities" on BLM-managed land. Prior to the initiation of the well stimulation activity, the lessee must obtain BLM approval for the well stimulation and must provide BLM with, among other things: a detailed description of the well stimulation engineering design, an estimate of the total amount of fluid to be used, an estimate of the total volume of fluid to be used and the maximum injection pressure anticipated, and information about the anticipated volume and handling of the flowback.[13]

---

[10] President Barack Obama, 2012 State of the Union Address (January 24, 2012), *available at* http://www.whitehouse.gov/photos-and-video/video/2012/01/25/2012-state-union-address-enhanced-version#transcript.

[11] *See, e.g.*, Interstate Oil and Gas Compact Commission, Hydraulic Fracturing, *available at* http://www.iogcc.state.ok.us/hydraulic-fracturing.

[12] Oil and Gas; Well Stimulation, Including Hydraulic Fracturing, on Federal and Indian Lands, 77 Fed. Reg. 27,691 (May 11, 2012).

[13] *Id.* at 27,696.

There do not appear to be disclosure requirements related to the chemical makeup of the fracturing fluid that the lessee plans to use prior to the well stimulation activity. However, after the completion of the activity, the proposed rule would require the lessee to "identify to the BLM the stimulation fluid by additive trade name and additive purpose, the Chemical Abstracts Service Registry Number, and the percent mass of each ingredient used in the stimulation operation."[14] BLM noted in the proposed rule that "[t]his information is needed in order for the BLM to maintain a record of the stimulation operation as performed. The information is being required in a format that does not link additives ... to chemical composition of the materials to minimize the risk of disclosure of any formulas of additives."[15] According to BLM, "[t]his approach is similar to the one the State of Colorado adopted in 2011."[16] The proposed rule also sets forth a number of other reporting requirements regarding the well stimulation operation upon completion of the operation.[17]

Legislation in the 112th Congress: The FRAC Act

On March 15, 2011, the Fracturing Responsibility and Awareness of Chemicals Act of 2011 (FRAC Act), H.R. 1084 and S. 587, was introduced in both the Senate and the House of Representatives. The bills have some minor language differences, but are substantially similar. (They also are similar to bills introduced in the past Congress.) Each contains two amendments to the Safe Drinking Water Act (SDWA)—one that would amend the definition of underground injection to include hydraulic fracturing, and another that would create a new disclosure requirement for the chemicals used in hydraulic fracturing.

The second amendment to the SDWA in the FRAC Act would create a new hydraulic fracturing disclosure requirement. H.R. 1084 would create a new statutory obligation requiring anyone conducting hydraulic fracturing to

> disclose to the State (or the Administrator [of the Environmental Protection Agency] if the Administrator has primary enforcement responsibility in the State)—(I) prior to the commencement of any hydraulic fracturing operations at any lease area or portion thereof, a list of chemicals intended for use in any underground injection during such operations, including identification of the chemical constituents of mixtures, Chemical Abstracts Service numbers for each chemical and constituent, material safety data sheets when available, and the anticipated volume of each chemical; and (II) not later than 30 days after the end of any hydraulic fracturing operations the list of chemicals used in each underground injection during such operations, including identification of the chemical constituents of mixtures, Chemical Abstracts Service numbers for each chemical and constituent, material safety data sheets when available, and the volume of each chemical used.[18]

The bill would also require that the state or the Environmental Protection Agency (EPA) "make the disclosure of chemical constituents ... available to the public, including by posting the information on an appropriate Internet Web site," and the bill clarifies that the disclosure requirements "do not authorize the State (or the [EPA]) to require the public disclosure of

---

[14] *Id.* at 27,698.

[15] *Id.*

[16] *Id.*

[17] *Id.*

[18] H.R. 1084, §2(b).

proprietary chemical formulas."[19] In other words, the disclosure requirements address only the chemicals used, not the manner of their use or the amounts or ratios in which they are used. This language attempts to protect proprietary business information, that is, "secret" formulas or practices that drilling companies may feel they should not be required to disclose to their competitors.

Furthermore, the FRAC Act would require operators to disclose proprietary chemical information to medical professionals in cases of medical emergencies.[20] Although most state oil and gas rules do not require disclosure of proprietary chemical information to medical professionals, such disclosure broadly parallels federal requirements under the Occupational Safety and Health Act (OSHAct).[21] Calls for disclosure of hydraulic fracturing chemicals have increased as homeowners and others express concern about the potential presence of unknown chemicals in tainted well water near oil and gas operations.

State Disclosure Laws

Of the states that produce oil, natural gas, or both, at least 15 require some disclosure of information about the chemicals added to the hydraulic fracturing fluid used to stimulate a particular well. State requirements, which take the form of laws, regulations, and administrative interpretations, vary widely. Generally, they fall into four overlapping categories: (1) which parties must disclose information about chemical additives and whether these disclosures must be made to the public or a state agency; (2) what information about chemicals added to a fracturing fluid must be disclosed, including how specifically parties must describe the chemical makeup of the fracturing fluid and the additives that are combined with it; (3) what protections, if any, will be given to trade secrets; and (4) at what time disclosure must be made in relation to when fracturing takes place. States update their laws on fracturing chemical disclosure frequently, and thus this section is designed to show trends in how states structure these provisions rather than to describe the current status of the law in any particular state. **Appendix A** provides a glossary of many of the terms used in this section. **Appendix B** contains a table summarizing the chemical disclosure requirements discussed in this report.

Who Must Make Disclosures and To Whom

State disclosure laws require at least one party involved in the hydraulic fracturing of a specific well to divulge information about the chemicals added to the fluid used to fracture that well. Under these laws, parties that must make disclosures include well owners, well operators, drilling

---

[19] *Id.*

[20] *Id.*

[21] The Occupational Safety and Health Administration has promulgated a set of regulations under Occupational Safety and Health Act (OSHAct), referred to as the Hazard Communication Standard (29 C.F.R. §1910.1200). Additionally, OSHAct regulations require operators to maintain Material Safety Data Sheets (MSDS) for hazardous chemicals at the job site. The federal Emergency Planning and Community Right to Know Act (EPCRA) requires that facility owners submit an MSDS for each hazardous chemical present that exceeds an EPA-determined threshold level, or a list of such chemicals, to the local emergency planning committee (LEPC), the state emergency response commission, and the local fire department. For non-proprietary information, EPCRA generally requires a LEPC to provide an MSDS to a member of the public on request.

permit holders, or "persons" that perform a fracturing treatment, such as service companies.[22] Parties typically must divulge chemical information to the public, a state agency, or both. States that require public disclosure often mandate that parties post the information on an Internet website such as the FracFocus Chemical Disclosure Registry run by the Groundwater Protection Council and the Interstate Oil and Gas Compact Commission.[23] Some state laws do not require direct public disclosure of fracturing chemicals. However, some state agencies may choose to post the information they receive on their own websites. Additionally, state open records laws may allow a person to obtain chemical information submitted to a state agency upon request, provided that the information is not shielded from disclosure by an exception, such as an exemption for trade secrets.[24]

Disclosure laws in at least four states require that chemical information be submitted directly to the public via posting of the information on the FracFocus Chemical Disclosure Registry or a comparable website.[25] By contrast, at least a couple of states give disclosing parties a choice as to whether they will submit the information to a state agency or post it on a website accessible to the public.[26] Several states where commercial natural gas exploration and production occur do not specifically provide for public disclosure, choosing instead to have parties submit details on chemical additives solely to state agencies, some of which may opt to post these disclosures to their websites.[27]

The particular parties involved in the fracturing of a well that must disclose chemical information to regulators or the public vary by state. In about half of the states with these laws, the operator of the well must disclose information about the chemicals used.[28] State laws that require disclosure

---

[22] Some states specifically provide for an intermediate stage of disclosure before the information is submitted to regulators or the public. *See, e.g.*, 178-00 Ark. Code R. §001:B-19(k), (l)(4) (person fracturing the well to permit holder); Colo. Code Regs. §404-1:205A(b)(1), (2) (certain service providers and vendors to operator); 58 Pa. Cons. Stat. §3222.1(b)(1), (2) (certain service providers and vendors to operator); 16 Tex. Admin. Code §3.29(c)(1)(A), (2)(A) (supplier or service company to operator).

[23] The website is located at http://fracfocus.org/.

[24] *See, e.g.*, Idaho Admin. Code r. 20.07.02.006 (providing for public disclosure of information submitted to the state unless it is exempt); Wyo. Code Rules and Regs. Oil Gen. §45(f) (stating that fracturing chemical information will be protected to the extent of the Wyoming Public Records Act's exemption for "trade secrets, privileged information and confidential commercial, financial, geological or geophysical data furnished by or obtained from any person.").

[25] Colo. Code Regs. §404-1:205A(b)(2); N.D. Admin. Code 43-02-03-27.1(1)(g), (2)(h); 58 Pa. Cons. Stat. §3222.1(b)(2) (for "unconventional" wells); Texas Admin. Code §3.29(c)(2)(A).

[26] Louisiana's regulation states that the operator must make disclosures to the state agency or "furnish a statement signifying that the required information has been submitted" to the FracFocus site or a comparable registry, so long as "all information is accessible to the public free of charge." La. Admin. Code tit. 43, §118(C)(1), (C)(4). For disclosures made after fracturing, the Montana Board of Oil and Gas may waive disclosure to the state if the owner or operator of the well "demonstrates that it has posted the required information" to FracFocus or another website that can be accessed by the public and meets with the state agency's approval. Mont. Admin. R. 36.22.1015(4).

[27] *See, e.g.*, 178-00 Ark. Code R. §001:B-19(k), (l)(3); Idaho Admin. Code r. 20.07.02.056; N.M. Admin. Code §19.15.16.19(B); W. Va. Code §22-6A-7(a)-(b), (e)(5); Wyo. Code Rules and Regs. Oil Gen. §45(d), (h); Michigan Department of Environmental Quality, Supervisor of Wells Instruction 1-2011, High Volume Hydraulic Fracturing Well Completions 3 (2011) [hereinafter Michigan Fracturing Instruction], *available at* http://www.michigan.gov/documents/deq/SI_1-2011_353936_7.pdf. For an example of a state's posting of chemical information to its website, see State of Arkansas Oil and Gas Commission, Well Fracture Information, http://www.aogc.state.ar.us/Well_Fracture_Companies.htm.

[28] *See, e.g.*, Colo. Code Regs. §404-1:205A(b)(2); La. Admin. Code tit. 43, §118(C)(1), (C)(4); N.M. Admin. Code §19.15.16.19(B); 58 Pa. Cons. Stat. §3222.1(b)(2); 16 Tex. Admin. Code §3.29(c)(2)(A); Michigan Fracturing Instruction, *supra* note 27, at 3.

---

by either the owner or operator of the well include Idaho[29] and Montana (after fracturing).[30] The operator, well owner, or service company must divulge chemical information in North Dakota[31] and Wyoming.[32] In Arkansas, any "person" fracturing a well in the state must disclose chemical information before fracturing, and the permit holder must divulge more detailed information afterward.[33]

What Must Be Disclosed

State disclosure laws require parties to provide various levels of detail about the chemical makeup of the fluid used in hydraulic fracturing. Because some states contain protections for trade secrets that may allow parties to withhold chemical information from regulators or the public, it may be difficult to compare the *actual* level of disclosure required.[34] Moreover, in a few states, decisions about what details are trade secrets exempt from disclosure are made by the state attorney general or a state agency. These decision makers may shield information from public disclosure at their discretion, typically subject to judicial review.[35] This section provides a few examples of state laws that require different levels of disclosure, but does not take into account the trade secret protections in those states. For a table showing the level of disclosure required on a state-by-state basis, see **Appendix B**.

The level of disclosure required by a particular law depends on how specifically parties must describe the chemical composition of the fracturing fluid and the additives that are combined with it. Some states require a relatively high level of disclosure, at least before trade secret protections are taken into account. For example, Colorado requires parties to identify each chemical ingredient in the overall fracturing fluid by its Chemical Abstracts Service (CAS) number[36] and to provide the maximum concentration of each ingredient within the fluid.[37] Other states require fewer details about the composition of a fracturing fluid. For example, West Virginia requires only that a list of additives be provided.[38] Between these two ends of the spectrum are rules such as Louisiana's, which obligates parties to provide the CAS numbers and maximum concentrations

---

[29] Idaho Admin. Code r. 20.07.02.056.

[30] *See* Mont. Admin. R. 36 22.1015(1), (4). The state also requires certain disclosures to be made by the operator before fracturing either in the drilling permit application or, in some circumstances, in a Sundry Notice. Mont. Admin. R. 36.22.608(1)-(2).

[31] N.D. Admin. Code 43-02-03-27.1(1)(g), (2)(h).

[32] Wyo. Code Rules and Regs. Oil Gen. §45(d), (h).

[33] 178-00 Ark. Code R. §001:B-19(k), (l)(3). In West Virginia, the permit applicant must make the disclosures before fracturing, and the operator must make them after fracturing. W. Va. Code §22-6A-7(a)-(b), (e)(5).

[34] For a discussion of these protections, see "Trade Secret Protections," *infra*. These protections may be contained in a state's disclosure law or, for disclosures made to state agencies, an exemption for trade secrets contained in a state's open records law.

[35] *See, e.g.*, 178-00 Ark. Code R. §001:B-19(k)(8), (l)(3)(C) (director of state agency); Texas Admin. Code §3.29(f) (state attorney general); Wyo. Code Rules and Regs. Oil Gen. §45(f) (state agency).

[36] For more about these numbers, see CAS Registry Numbers, http://www.cas.org/expertise/cascontent/registry/regsys.html.

[37] Colo. Code Regs. §404-1:205A(b)(2)(A)(ix)-(xii). It does not require parties to link the ingredients to the additive of which they are a part.

[38] *See, e.g.*, W. Va. Code §22-6A-7(e)(5). Other information that may provide a relatively low level of disclosure includes information such as additive type (for example, acid, biocide, or breaker); trade name or vendor of an additive; or volume of an additive. *See, e.g.*, La. Admin. Code tit. 43, §118(C)(1)(a)-(c) (requiring some of these characteristics but also requiring a higher level of disclosure for hazardous ingredients).

of hazardous ingredients present in the fluid, but not nonhazardous ingredients.[39] At least four states require disclosures to be made before and after fracturing. In these states, the level of disclosure differs depending on whether the information is submitted before or after treatment of the well.[40]

Some states require that parties submit Material Safety Data Sheets (MSDSs) for additives or chemical ingredients in a fracturing fluid.[41] Employers are required to use MSDSs to warn employees of hazardous chemicals in the workplace under the OSHAct.[42] Because MSDSs provide data only on chemicals considered to be hazardous under OSHA regulations, they may offer a relatively low level of disclosure.[43] The most specific details that parties must include on MSDSs are the common or chemical names of certain hazardous ingredients, assuming that the names do not qualify for trade secret protection.[44] Thus, under the regulations, CAS numbers or the concentrations of ingredients within an additive do not have to be listed.[45] This does not mean, however, that some parties would not voluntarily submit data sheets with more information.

A few states specifically exempt certain information from disclosure. In Colorado, a party is not required to

> (1) disclose chemicals that are not disclosed to it by the manufacturer, vendor, or service provider; (2) disclose chemicals that were not intentionally added to the hydraulic fracturing fluid; or (3) disclose chemicals that occur incidentally or are otherwise unintentionally present in trace amounts, may be the incidental result of a chemical reaction or chemical process, or may be constituents of naturally occurring materials that become part of a hydraulic fracturing fluid.[46]

Laws in Pennsylvania[47] and Texas[48] contain similar language.

---

[39] La. Admin. Code tit. 43, §118(C)(1)(d)-(e). The Louisiana rule states that this information must be provided for "ingredients contained in the hydraulic fracturing fluid that are subject to the requirements of 29 CFR Section 1910.1200(g)(2)." In other words, the information must be provided for those ingredients that are hazardous according to OSHA's regulation on workplace hazard communication.

[40] These states include Arkansas (more detail afterward), Idaho (less detail afterward), Montana (more detail afterward), and Wyoming (less detail afterward). *See* 178-00 Ark. Code R. §001:B-19(k)(7)-(8), (l)(3)(C); Idaho Admin. Code r. 20.07.02.056; Mont. Admin. R. 36.22.608, 36.22.1015; Wyo. Code Rules and Regs. Oil Gen. §45(d), (h).

[41] *See, e.g.*, Michigan Fracturing Instruction, *supra* note 27, at 3. *See also* N.M. Admin. Code §19.15.16.19(B) (stating that the operator does not have to report any more information than is required to be reported on MSDSs under OSHA regulations on hazard communication in the workplace).

[42] *See* 29 C.F.R. §1910.1200(a)(1).

[43] OSHA recently modified its Hazard Communication Standard, effective May 25, 2012. The regulation now requires that by June 1, 2015, employers communicate workplace hazards to employees by using "safety data sheets" that are consistent with the United Nations Globally Harmonized System of Classification and Labeling of Chemicals. 29 C.F.R. §1910.1200(a), (j). In addition to other information, the data sheets will be required to contain a more specific description of certain chemical substances and mixtures, provided that this information does not qualify for trade secret protection under the regulations. 29 C.F.R. §1910.1200(g), (i), app. D. During the transition period, parties may comply with the new regulations, the previous version of the regulations, or both. 29 C.F.R. §1910.1200(j)(3).

[44] *See id.* §1910.1200(g)(2), (i) (2011).

[45] *See id.*

[46] Colo. Code Regs. §404-1:205A(c).

[47] 58 Pa. Cons. Stat. §3222.1(c).

Trade Secret Protections

Closely related to *what* must be submitted under a particular disclosure law are the protections provided for trade secrets. More than half of the disclosure laws examined contain trade secret protections. A state may require detailed disclosure of chemical information, but if it also provides a high degree of protection for trade secrets, parties may be able to avoid making significant disclosures to a state agency or the public. Although the definition of a "trade secret" may differ under various states' laws, this section assumes that a trade secret is: (a) information valuable to its owner because others who could obtain value from it do not know the information and cannot easily discover it; and (b) information that is subject to reasonable measures to protect it from disclosure.[49] Whether a particular law requires the public disclosure of trade secrets may have implications for whether a court would find that the law effects a taking of property under the Takings Clause of the Fifth Amendment—a finding that could potentially require that just compensation be made to the owner of the trade secrets.[50]

A couple of disclosure laws lack trade secret protections. These include Michigan's and West Virginia's. States may not provide trade secret protections because the information required to be disclosed under their laws is not detailed enough to be considered a trade secret, perhaps because it is knowledge that is generally known or easily discoverable.[51] Or, in some instances, trade secret protections may be provided in another state law, such as an exemption for trade secrets contained in an open records law that could allow a state agency that had received chemical information to prevent it from being disclosed to the public.[52]

At least one state allows parties to withhold all details about fracturing additives that the parties consider to be trade secrets. New Mexico's rule states, "The division does not require the reporting or disclosure of proprietary, trade secret or confidential business information," apparently leaving the determination of what may be excluded to the discretion of the submitter.[53] In contrast, a few states allow withholding only if parties provide alternative information about chemical ingredients to regulators or the public for disclosure, such as the chemical family for the ingredients. For example, Montana asks that, for withheld trade secret chemicals, parties provide the "trade name, inventory name, chemical family name, or other unique name and the quantity of such constituent(s) used."[54] In Montana,[55] as well as in Colorado[56] and Louisiana,[57] when parties

---

(...continued)

[48] 16 Tex. Admin. Code §3.29(d).

[49] *See* U.T.S.A. §1(4) (1985). A few states continue to rely on the definition provided in the Restatement of Torts, §757 cmt. b (1939). Texas provides a definition of "trade secret" within its chemical disclosure law that is based on the Restatement definition. 16 Tex. Admin. Code §3.29(a)(26).

[50] *See generally* Ruckelshaus v. Monsanto, 467 U.S. 986 (1984) (holding that when the government discloses trade secrets that a party has been required to submit to the government by law, a taking could result in some circumstances); Philip Morris v. Reilly, 312 F.3d 24 (1st Cir. 2002) (en banc) (holding that a law that compels disclosure of a party's trade secrets may effect a taking).

[51] *See supra* sources cited note 49; *see also Philip Morris*, 312 F.3d at 27 (lead opinion) (discussing how companies challenging a disclosure law feared that the disclosure of the relative amounts of ingredients in their products would allow competitors to reverse engineer the chemical formulas for them).

[52] *See, e.g.*, Wyo. Code Rules and Regs. Oil Gen. §45(f).

[53] N.M. Admin. Code §19.15.16.19(B).

[54] Mont. Admin. R. 36 22.1016.

[55] *Id.*

[56] Colo. Code Regs. §404-1:205A(b)(2)(B)-(C), (d).

withhold information and provide a less detailed description of chemical additives, it does not appear that regulators have the authority to compel further disclosure in ordinary circumstances.[58] However, as described below, some states make an exception and require disclosure in special circumstances like spills or medical emergencies.

Some disclosure laws give the state attorney general or a state agency the authority to approve or deny an exemption for trade secrets. These laws vary as to whether parties may withhold the information prior to the decision or must first submit it to the state. For example, the Texas rule, which allows parties to initially withhold information, allows landowners and others to challenge a claim of trade secret protection and lists procedures to be used by the state attorney general to decide whether to exempt the information from disclosure.[59] Arkansas's rule states that parties may withhold the information and submit a claim for a trade secret exemption to the state agency.[60] The agency decides whether information qualifies for protection under the criteria provided in the federal Emergency Planning and Community Right-to-Know Act.[61] In Wyoming, the state oil and gas commission decides whether information that has been submitted to it is exempt from public disclosure under the Wyoming Public Records Act.[62]

At least seven disclosure laws make an exception to trade secret protections for situations in which a health care professional needs the information in order to provide medical care. Typically, the professional must execute a confidentiality agreement before or after disclosure occurs.[63] For example, Colorado's rule states the following:

> Vendors, service companies, and operators shall identify the specific identity and amount of any chemicals claimed to be a trade secret to any health professional who requests such information in writing if the health professional provides a written statement of need for the information and executes a confidentiality agreement, Form 35. The written statement of need shall be a statement that the health professional has a reasonable basis to believe that (1) the information is needed for purposes of diagnosis or treatment of an individual, (2) the individual being diagnosed or treated may have been exposed to the chemical concerned, and (3) knowledge of the information will assist in such diagnosis or treatment.[64]

(...continued)

[57] La. Admin. Code tit. 43, §118(C)(2)(a).

[58] It is possible that another state law or regulation may provide an avenue for some parties to compel disclosure. For example, the Colorado Oil and Gas Conservation Commission maintains that a party wishing to challenge a trade secret claim could bring a lawsuit under a provision in the state's Oil and Gas Conservation Act or file a complaint under a certain commission rule. The agency would then decide whether to "receive, investigate, assess and determine claims that a vendor, service company or operator has improperly claimed a trade secret" or whether to allow a court to decide the issue. *See* COGCC, Proposed Statement of Basis, Specific Statutory Authority, and Purpose, http://cogcc.state.co.us/RR_HF2011/Order1R-114FinalFracingDisclosureRule.pdf (see pages 12-13).

[59] 16 Tex. Admin. Code §3.29(e)-(f).

[60] 178-00 Ark. Code R. §001:B-19(k)(8), (l)(3)(C).

[61] *Id.; see also* 42 U.S.C. § 11042(a)(2).

[62] Wyo. Code Rules and Regs. Oil Gen. §45(f) (referring to a provision in the Wyoming Public Records Act). The party claiming trade secret protection must justify and document the "nature and extent of the proprietary information." Idaho provides a similar kind of protection to trade secrets. *See* Idaho Admin. Code r. 20.07.02.006.

[63] This may be intended to ensure that a disclosing party preserves any trade secrets disclosed, as trade secrets may be destroyed if revealed to a third party without a confidentiality agreement. *See* sources cited *supra* note 49.

[64] Colo. Code Regs. §404-1:205A(b)(5).

In addition, Colorado's rule provides that in immediate medical emergencies, trade secret information must be provided to the health professional "upon a verbal acknowledgement by the health professional that such information shall not be used for purposes other than the health needs asserted and that the health professional shall otherwise maintain the information as confidential."[65] A written confidentiality agreement may be requested "as soon as circumstances permit."[66] Other states with some form of medical emergency exception include Arkansas (confidentiality agreement not required in rule),[67] Idaho (confidentiality agreement not required in rule),[68] Louisiana (confidentiality agreement not required in rule),[69] Montana (confidentiality agreement may be required in non-emergencies; may be requested in emergencies),[70] Pennsylvania (written confidentiality agreement required in non-emergencies; may be requested in emergencies when circumstances permit),[71] and Texas (information must be held confidential).[72] Colorado's rule provides a similar kind of exception for disclosures provided to state agency employees responding to a spill or release, with provisions for confidentiality,[73] as do similar provisions in states such as Montana[74] and Pennsylvania.[75]

When Disclosures Must Be Made

A few states mandate disclosures both before and after each fracturing treatment. For example, prior to fracturing in Wyoming, a party must disclose "for each stage of the well stimulation program, the chemical additives, compounds and concentrations or rates *proposed* to be mixed and injected."[76] After the procedure, at least one of the applicable parties must disclose information about the *actual* chemicals used.[77] Similar rules exist in states such as Arkansas,[78] Idaho,[79] and Montana,[80] which require that disclosures made after fracturing contain a different level of detail than those made before fracturing.

Disclosures made prior to fracturing that specifically identify the chemicals that will be used potentially give parties with access to the data the opportunity to perform baseline testing on

---

[65] *Id.*

[66] *Id.*

[67] 178-00 Ark. Code R. §001:B-19(k)(9), (l)(5). A couple of states' exceptions provide that trade secrets must be disclosed in emergencies when state or federal law requires disclosure. *See, e.g.,* 178-00 Ark. Code R. §001:B-19(k)(9), (l)(5); La. Admin. Code tit. 43, §118(C)(3).

[68] Idaho Admin. Code r. 20.07.02.200.

[69] La. Admin. Code tit. 43, §118(C)(3).

[70] Mont. Admin. R. 36 22.1016(3)-(4).

[71] Pa. Cons. Stat. §3222.1(b)(10)-(11). If a confidentiality agreement is requested, the health professional must provide one.

[72] 16 Tex. Admin. Code §3.29(c)(4), (g). The Texas rule borrows some of its confidentiality procedures from OSHA's regulations on hazard communication at 29 C.F.R. §1910.1200(i). 16 Tex. Admin. Code §3.29(c)(4).

[73] Colo. Code Regs. §404-1:205A(d).

[74] Mont. Admin. R. 36 22.1016(2).

[75] Pa. Cons. Stat. §3222.1(d)(2).

[76] Wyo. Code Rules and Regs. Oil Gen. §45(d).

[77] *Id.* §45(h).

[78] 178-00 Ark. Code R. §001:B-19(k), (l)(3).

[79] Idaho Admin. Code r. 20.07.02.056.

[80] Mont. Admin. R. 36 22.608, 36.22.1015.

---

water sources near the drilling site for those particular chemicals.[81] Baseline testing results can then be compared with results from post-well stimulation testing to see if any groundwater contamination has occurred and, if it has, to possibly locate its source.[82] Proponents of pre-fracturing disclosure have argued that, among other things, it would: (1) provide landowners with the identities of the chemicals they should test for when they collect baseline water samples prior to drilling; and (2) assist emergency personnel and health professionals in responding to a spill or release by providing them with information about the identities of the chemicals that were used in the fluid.[83]

However, some in the industry have argued that requiring an operator to disclose chemical information prior to hydraulic fracturing is of questionable value and does not comport with realities in the field. Arguments to this effect include: (1) the chemical composition of the fracturing fluid is often continually adjusted prior to treatment of the well, and so disclosures made prior to fracturing may not accurately reflect the actual chemicals that will be used; and (2) requiring the operator to gather chemical information from its contractors and report the information to regulators may slow down production.[84]

Other state disclosure laws require parties to submit information about the chemicals used to fracture a well at a single time following the drilling, fracturing, or completion of the well. States with laws that require disclosure after completion of a well that has been fractured include Louisiana (within 20 days),[85] New Mexico (within 45 days),[86] and Texas (timeframe varies).[87] Ohio law mandates disclosures within 60 days after completion of the drilling of the well to the "proposed total depth" or "after a determination that a well is a dry or lost hole."[88] Colorado,[89]

---

[81] American Petroleum Institute, Hydraulic Fracturing Operations—Well Construction and Integrity Guidelines §10.2 (2009), *available at* http://www.api.org/~/media/Files/Policy/Exploration/API_HF1.ashx. For more information on this issue, see CRS Report R41760, *Hydraulic Fracturing and Safe Drinking Water Act Issues*, by Mary Tiemann and Adam Vann.

[82] *See* sources cited *supra* note 81.

[83] *See, e.g.*, Western Colorado Congress Prehearing Statement p. 3, http://cogcc.state.co.us/RR_HF2011/PrehearingStatements/WesternColoradoCongress_PHS.pdf. *See also* Katarzyna Klimasinska, *Drillers May Frack First, Disclose Later Under Draft Plan*, http://www.bloomberg.com/news/2012-05-01/drillers-may-frack-first-disclose-later-under-draft-plan.html.

[84] Some of these arguments were raised during the Colorado rulemaking. *See, e.g.*, Joint Rebuttal Statement of the Colorado Petroleum Association and Colorado Oil & Gas Association p. 7, http://cogcc.state.co.us/RR_HF2011/RebuttalStatements/ColoradoPetroleumAssoc-ColoradoOilGassAssoc_Joint_RS.PDF; Western Colorado Congress Rebuttal Statement pp. 7-9, http://cogcc.state.co.us/RR_HF2011/RebuttalStatements/WesternColoradoCongress_RS.PDF.

[85] La. Admin. Code tit. 43, §118(C)(1) (referring to La. Admin. Code tit. 43, §105 for the timeframe).

[86] N.M. Admin. Code §19.15.16.19(B).

[87] In Texas, the operator must divulge chemicals to the public "on or before the date the well completion report" is sent to the state agency. 16 Tex. Admin. Code §3.29(c)(2)(A). Well completion reports are due on the earlier date of 30 days after well completion or 90 days after drilling is finished. *Id.* §3.16(b).

[88] Ohio Rev. Code §1509.10(A). "If a well is not completed within sixty days after the completion of drilling operations," the owner must file a "supplemental well completion record" with the pertinent information "within sixty days after the completion of the well." *Id.* §1509.10(B)(2). West Virginia requires disclosures to be made with a report that must be filed within a "reasonable time" after drilling. W. Va. Code §22-6A-7(e)(5); *see also id.* §22-6-22(a).

[89] Colo. Code Regs. §404-1:205A(b)(2). However, Colorado's rule also specifies that disclosure must be made no later than 120 days after fracturing begins.

North Dakota,[90] Oklahoma,[91] and Pennsylvania[92] require disclosure within 60 days after a fracturing treatment ends.

Conclusion

Many federal and state legislators and regulatory authorities have adopted or proposed measures that would create new disclosure requirements applicable to the practice of hydraulic fracturing, a natural resource recovery technique that is widely used in the recovery of natural gas from shale formations. The Shale Gas Production Subcommittee of the Secretary of Energy Advisory Board has recommended the public disclosure, on a well-by-well basis, of all of the chemical ingredients added to fracturing fluids—even those ingredients that do not meet OSHA's standards for hazardous chemicals requiring MSDSs. The subcommittee recommended that some protection for trade secrets be provided.

At the federal level, BLM has proposed disclosure requirements that would be applicable for hydraulic fracturing on all lands managed by the agency. Legislation has been introduced in the 112th Congress that would create disclosure requirements for all hydraulic fracturing operations nationally.

Chemical disclosure laws at the state level vary widely. Of the 15 laws examined in this report, fewer than half require direct public disclosure of chemical information by mandating that parties post the information on the FracFocus chemical disclosure website. The level of detail required to be disclosed often depends on how states protect trade secrets, as these protections may allow submitting parties to withhold information from disclosure at their discretion or to submit fewer details about proprietary chemicals, except, perhaps, in emergencies. Even if a disclosure law does not protect information from public disclosure, other state laws, such as an exemption in an open records law, may do so. A few states require the submission of MSDSs for certain chemicals. MSDSs may offer a relatively low level of disclosure, as the most specific details that parties currently must include on the data sheets under OSHA regulations are the chemical or common names of certain hazardous ingredients. With regard to the timing of disclosure, a few state laws require at least some disclosure of information about fracturing fluid chemical composition before fracturing is performed, but these states typically require less detailed information to be provided before fracturing than afterward.

---

[90] N.D. Admin. Code 43-02-03-27.1(1)(g), (2)(h).

[91] Okla. Admin. Code § 165: 10-3-10(b).

[92] 58 Pa. Cons. Stat. §3222.1(b)(2).

Appendix A. Glossary of Terms

Additive	A product composed of one or more chemical constituents that is added to a primary carrier fluid to modify its properties in order to form hydraulic fracturing fluid
Chemical Abstracts Service (CAS) Number	The unique identification number assigned to a chemical by the division of the American Chemical Society that is the globally recognized authority for information on chemical substances
Chemical Constituent/Ingredient	A discrete chemical with its own specific name or identity, such as a CAS number, that is contained in an additive
Chemical Family	A group of chemicals that share certain physical and chemical characteristics and have a common general name
Completion	The activities and methods used to prepare a well for production after drilling
FracFocus.org	The chemical disclosure registry website developed by the Ground Water Protection Council and the Interstate Oil and Gas Compact Commission
Hydraulic Fracturing	The treatment of a well by the application of hydraulic fracturing fluid under pressure for the express purpose of initiating or propagating fractures in a target geologic formation to enhance production of oil and/or natural gas
Hydraulic Fracturing Fluid	The primary carrier fluid and all applicable additives
Material Safety Data Sheet (MSDS)	A written or printed document that is prepared for a chemical mixture or ingredient considered to be hazardous under OSHA standards according to OSHA's regulations on hazard communication at 29 C.F.R. §1910.1200(g)(2)
Operator	A person who assumes responsibility for the physical operation and control of a well
Owner	A person who owns, manages, leases, controls, or possesses a well property
Primary Carrier Fluid	The base fluid, such as water, into which additives are mixed to form the hydraulic fracturing fluid that transports proppant
Product	A hydraulic fracturing additive that is manufactured using precise amounts of specific chemical constituents and is assigned a commercial name under which the substance is sold or utilized
Proppant	Sand or any natural or man-made material that is used in a hydraulic fracturing treatment to prop open the artificially created or enhanced fractures once the treatment is completed
Service Company	An entity that performs hydraulic fracturing treatments on a well
Supplier	A company that sells or provides an additive for use in a hydrauic fracturing treatment
Trade Secret	Any formula, pattern, device, or compilation of information that is used in a person's business, and that gives the person an opportunity to obtain an advantage over competitors who do not know or use it

Source: Compiled by the Congressional Research Service from definitions contained in the Department of Energy's primer on shale gas development; the Arkansas, Pennsylvania, and Texas disclosure laws or regulations; and New York's proposed disclosure rule.

Note: This glossary provides common definitions for terms found in the report. A particular law may define these terms differently.

Appendix B. Summary of Chemical Disclosure Laws

Table B-1. Hydraulic Fracturing Chemical Disclosure Requirements

Laws and Proposals at the State and Federal Levels

Law (or Proposal)	Who Must Disclose and To Whom[a]	What Must Be Disclosed[b]	Trade Secret Protections[c]	When Disclosures Must Be Made
Proposed Bureau of Land Management Rule (would apply on lands managed by BLM)	Operator discloses to BLM. The agency intends to have the information posted on the FracFocus website.	Total volume of fluid; trade name and purpose of additive products; and CAS numbers of chemical ingredients and their concentrations (% by mass) in the entire fluid.	Operator could claim that a federal law or regulation protected information from disclosure but must explain why information is exempt. BLM would evaluate operator's claim.	Within 30 days after fracturing in the Subsequent Report Sundry Notice.
FRAC Act (S. 587; H.R. 1084)	Person conducting fracturing operations discloses to state (or EPA, if it has primary enforcement responsibility in the state), which posts on Internet.	Before and after fracturing: CAS numbers of ingredients in fracturing fluid; Material Safety Data Sheets when available; and "chemical" volumes.	No public disclosure of chemical formulas. Disclosure to state (or EPA) or health professional upon request in a medical emergency. Fracturing party may require confidentiality agreement after disclosure.	S. 587: before and after fracturing (same level of disclosure); deadlines set by state (or EPA). H.R. 1084: before fracturing and within 30 days after the end of fracturing (same level of disclosure).
Arkansas	Disclosures are made to state agency. Any "person" fracturing a well in the state makes less detailed disclosures before fracturing, and the permit holder makes more detailed disclosures after fracturing.	Before fracturing: disclosures include a list of additives; and names and CAS numbers of ingredients in fracture fluid. After fracturing: disclosures include the "types and volumes" of fluid and proppant used for each stage; additive names and types; names and CAS numbers of ingredients added to the fracture fluid by any person fracturing the well and the permit holder; and actual additive rates or concentrations (% by volume) in the fluid.	Chemical families must be provided when ingredient identities are withheld. A person fracturing a well and/or the permit holder may submit claim of protection to state agency for decision. Exceptions provided for situations in which state or federal law requires disclosure to a health professional.	Some disclosures before fracturing. More detailed disclosures must be made within 30 days of completion of a fractured well.

Law (or Proposal)	Who Must Disclose and To Whom[a]	What Must Be Disclosed[b]	Trade Secret Protections[c]	When Disclosures Must Be Made
Colorado	Operator discloses to the public by posting on the FracFocus website.	Total volume of water or other base fluid used during all stages of the operation; trade name, vendor, and purpose of each additive product used; the identity, CAS number, and maximum concentration (% by mass) of each ingredient intentionally added to the fluid.	Operator may designate information as a trade secret and withhold it but must submit the chemical family or similar descriptor. Claim submitted to state agency by vendor, service provider, or operator. Rule does not provide for evaluation of claims. Exceptions for medical emergencies and spills (with confidentia ity protections).	Within 60 days after fracturing ends but no later than 120 days after it begins.
Idaho	Before fracturing: owner or operator discloses to state in Application for Permit to Drill. After fracturing: owner or operator discloses to state in post-treatment report.	Before fracturing: disclosures include, for each stage, "chemical additives and proppant(s) and concentrations or rates proposed to be mixed and injected," including type, name, and CAS number of "additives" from Material Safety Data Sheets and "the formulary disclosure of the chemical compounds used in the well stimulation(s)." After fracturing: disclosures include concentrations (% by volume) of the base treatment fluid, individual "additives," and proppant(s) in the entire fracturing fluid.	Party may claim trade secret protection when it discloses to the state. Information is protected from pub ic disclosure to the extent of the state's public records law's exemption for trade secrets. Exception for when state or federal law requires disclosure to health professional.	Before fracturing in the Application for Permit to Drill. Within 30 days of fracturing in post-treatment report.

Law (or Proposal)	Who Must Disclose and To Whom[a]	What Must Be Disclosed[b]	Trade Secret Protections[c]	When Disclosures Must Be Made
Indiana (emergency instruction for coal bed methane wells)	Before fracturing: well permit applicant discloses to state. After fracturing: operator discloses to state.	Before fracturing: disclosures include proposed volume of base stimulation fluid; "proposed rate or concentration" of each additive product and a Material Safety Data Sheet for each product, if one exists. After fracturing: disclosures include volume of "base stimulation fluids" used; trade name and "rate or concentration" of each additive product; and Material Safety Data Sheets for products if not already submitted.	None in the emergency rule.	Before fracturing in the well permit application. After fracturing in the well completion or recompletion report.
Louisiana	Operator makes disclosures to state agency or submits statement that it has disclosed information to the public via FracFocus or a comparable website that is accessible to the public and free of charge.	Disclosures include: CAS numbers of ingredients and maximum ingredient concentrations within additives (% by mass) and within the fracture fluid (% by mass of total volume) of hazardous ingredients (under OSHA standards). Operator is not required to disclose information not disclosed to it by an entity claiming trade secret protection.	Chemical identities and CAS numbers may be withheld if claimed to be trade secrets or found to be trade secrets under 29 C.F.R. §1910.1200(i). Chemical family must still be provided. Exception in medical emergencies when state or federal law requires disclosure.	Within 20 days after well completion.
Michigan	Operator makes disclosures to state agency when it conducts a high-volume fracturing well completion.	Material Safety Data Sheets that are provided by service company for "additives" used; and volumes of additives.	None in the instruction.	Filed with record of well completion operations, which is due within 60 days of well completion.

Law (or Proposal)	Who Must Disclose and To Whom[a]	What Must Be Disclosed[b]	Trade Secret Protections[c]	When Disclosures Must Be Made
Montana	Before fracturing: operator discloses to state agency in drilling permit application or notice. After fracturing: owner or operator discloses to the state agency or public. Public disclosure occurs on FracFocus or other pubicly accessible website approved by the state agency.	Before fracturing: disclosures include "estimated total volume of treatment to be used"; trade name or generic name of "principal components or chemicals"; and the "estimated amount or volume of the principal components." After fracturing: types of additives used and their "rates or concentrations" in the fluid; and names and CAS numbers of the additives' chemical ingredients.	Owner, operator, or service contractor may withhold trade secret chemical and identify it by trade name, inventory name, chemical family, etc. and provide the quantity used. Exceptions for medical emergencies and spills (with confidentiaity protections).	Less specific disclosures made before fracturing in drilling permit application or notice. More specific disclosures made after fracturing upon completion of the well.
New Mexico	Operator discloses to state agency. Operator must certify that disclosures are true and complete to the best of its knowledge and belief.	Total volume of fluid; trade name, supplier, purpose, and CAS numbers of ingredients in fluid; and maximum concentrations of ingredients in additives and fluid (% by mass). However, no more disclosure must be made than would be included on a Material Safety Data Sheet under 29 C.F.R. §1910.1200.	"The division does not require the reporting or disclosure of proprietary, trade secret, or confidential business information."	Within 45 days after well completion.
North Dakota	Owner, operator, or service company discloses to the public on the FracFocus website.	"All elements made viewable by the FracFocus website."	Viewable elements on the FracFocus site do not include chemical information that submitting parties have withheld because it qualifies for trade secret protection under 29 C.F.R. §1910.1200(i)(1).	Within 60 days after fracturing.

Law (or Proposal)	Who Must Disclose and To Whom[a]	What Must Be Disclosed[b]	Trade Secret Protections[c]	When Disclosures Must Be Made
Ohio	Well owner makes disclosures in well completion record submitted to state agency or by posting information on FracFocus. State agency posts certain submitted chemical information on its website.	Disclosures include: the trade name and volume of all "products, fluids, and substances"; maximum concentrations of additives in the fluid; and CAS numbers and maximum concentrations of ingredients intentionally added to the fluid.	Owner (or party that discloses to owner) may withhold information considered to be trade secret information and pursue remedies for its misappropriation. Trade secret challenge is available in court to some parties. Exceptions exist for medical emergencies, spills, and investigations (with confidentiality protections).	Within 60 days after the end of drilling operations or after determination that well is a dry or lost hole. If the well is not completed within 60 days of drilling, owner must file a supplement with the information required within 60 days after well completion.
Oklahoma (applies to the fracturing of horizontal wells beginning in 2013 and other wells in 2014)	Operator discloses to FracFocus or the state agency. If submitted to state, the agency posts on FracFocus.	Disclosures include: total volume and type of base fluid; and CAS numbers and maximum concentrations (% by mass in fluid) of ingredients intentionally added.	Parties may "in good faith" withhold chemical information. Chemical family or similar descriptor must be provided if identity and CAS number are withheld. Parties may have to explain claim to state.	Within 60 days after fracturing.
Pennsylvania (requirements specific to "unconventional" wells)	Operator discloses to public on FracFocus. By Jan. 1, 2013, state agency determines whether FracFocus can be searched or sorted by CAS number, operator, geographic area, etc. If not, then agency must consider posting data on its website so data can be searched and sorted.	Operators make the disclosures required to be made on the FracFocus chemical disclosure form. Ingredients cannot be inked to additives. Disclosures not required are chemicals not disclosed by vendor, service provider, or operator; and chemicals not intentionally added to fracture fluid, etc.	Vendor, service provider, or operator may withhold trade secrets from pub ic. Operator discloses chemical family or similar descriptor. Medical emergency/spill exceptions (with confidentia ity protections) provided.	Within 60 days after fracturing.

Law (or Proposal)	Who Must Disclose and To Whom[a]	What Must Be Disclosed[b]	Trade Secret Protections[c]	When Disclosures Must Be Made
Texas	Operator discloses to public on FracFocus website.	Disclosures include: CAS numbers and actual/maximum concentrations (% by mass) of hazardous ingredients (according to OSHA standards) in fracture fluid. Also, CAS numbers for nonhazardous ingredients intentionally put in fracture fluid must be disclosed. Disclosures not required include chemicals not disclosed by manufacturer, supplier, or service company; and chemicals naturally occurring in fluid.	Supplier, service company, or operator may claim trade secret protection. Chemical family or similar description must be provided for chemicals withheld. Certain landowners and others may challenge trade secret claims. State attorney general decides if information is protected, subject to appeal. Exceptions for emergencies; borrows some confidentiaity procedures from 29 C.F.R. §1910.1200(i).	On or before the date the well completion report is due (timeframe varies).
West Virginia	Horizontal well work: permit applicant (before fracturing) and operator (after fracturing) disclose to state agency.	Before fracturing: list of anticipated "additives" that may be used. After fracturing: list of "additives" actually used submitted with well completion log.	None in the disclosure law.	Before fracturing: list of anticipated "additives" that may be used. After fracturing: list of "additives" actually used submitted with well completion log.
Wyoming	Owner, operator, or service company discloses to state agency.	Before fracturing: for each stage pumped, disclosures must include "the chemical additives, compounds and concentrations or rates proposed to be mixed and injected." After fracturing: disclosures must include the total volume of fluid pumped and, for each stage, the "actual chemical additive name, type, concentration or rate, and amounts."	Claim made to state agency. Trade secrets protected to extent of state open records law's exemption for trade secrets. Agency decides whether information is exempt from public disclosure.	Before and after fracturing.

Source: Compiled by the Congressional Research Service from the BLM proposed rule, FRAC Act, and state regulations.

Note: States update their laws on fracturing chemical disclosure frequently, and thus this table is designed to show trends in how states structure these provisions rather than to describe the current status of the law in any particular state.

a. This category does not include intermediate disclosures required to be made in some states, including Arkansas (person fracturing the well to permit holder), Colorado (certain service providers and vendors to operator), Pennsylvania (certain service providers and vendors to operator), and Texas (supplier or service company to operator). When disclosures are made to a government agency, some agencies may choose to disclose information to the public, for example by posting the information on their websites.

b. To determine the actual level of disclosure required, trade secret protections must be considered, as these protections may allow parties to prevent the disclosure of information to regulators or the pub ic.

c. This category refers only to trade secret protections contained in the disclosure law itse f and not in other laws that may provide protections, such as open records laws.

Author Contact Information

Brandon J. Murrill
Legislative Attorney
bmurrill@crs.loc.gov, 7-8440

Adam Vann
Legislative Attorney
avann@crs.loc.gov, 7-6978